Extreme Scientists

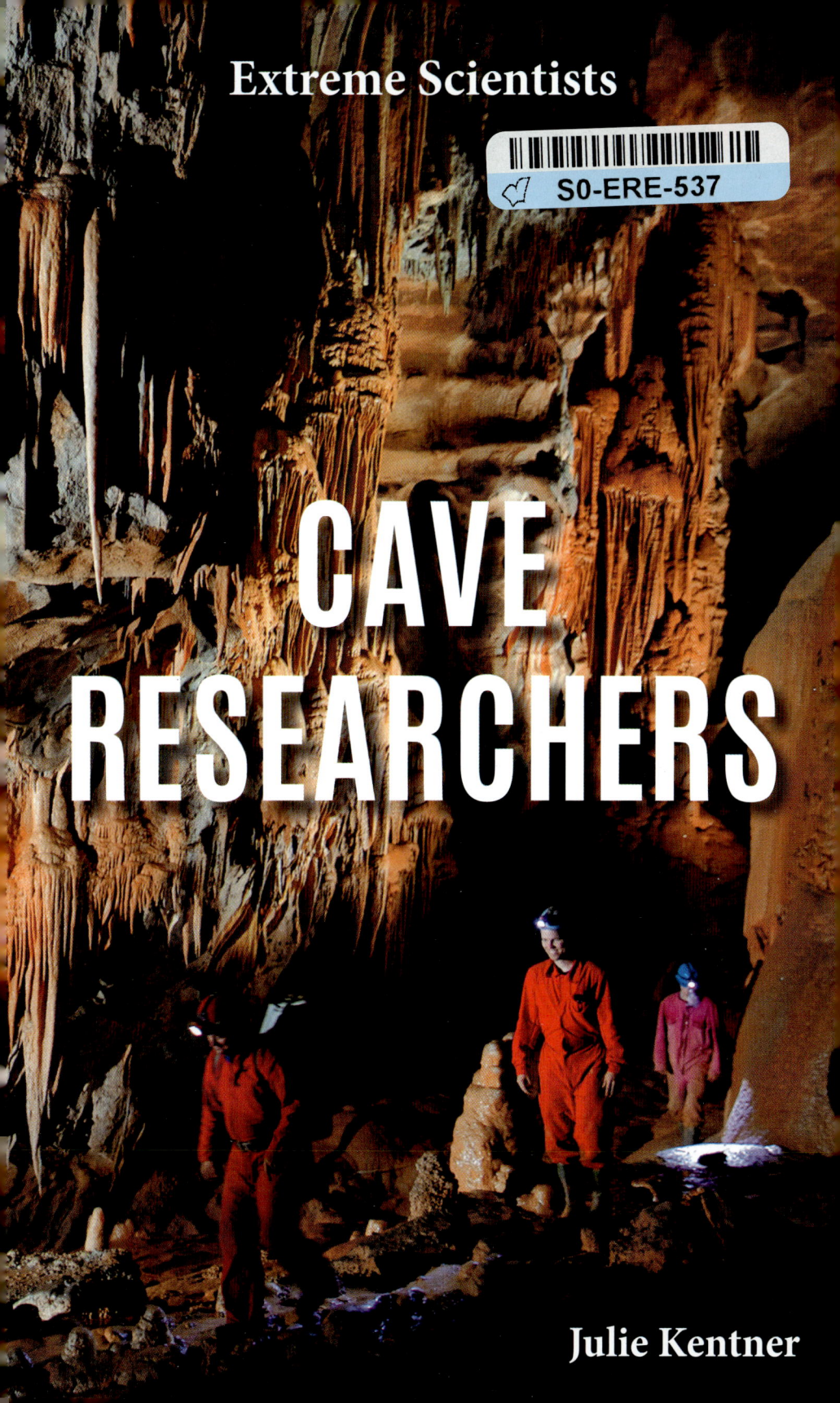

CAVE RESEARCHERS

Julie Kentner

WWW.APEXEDITIONS.COM

Copyright © 2025 by Apex Editions, Mendota Heights, MN 55120. All rights reserved. No part of this book may be reproduced or utilized in any form or by any means without written permission from the publisher.

Apex is distributed by North Star Editions:
sales@northstareditions.com | 888-417-0195

Produced for Apex by Red Line Editorial.

Photographs ©: iStockphoto, cover, 1, 10–11, 42–43, 44–45, 50–51, 52–53, 56–57, 58; Shutterstock Images, 4–5, 6–7, 14–15, 16–17, 18–19, 20–21, 22–23, 30–31, 54–55, 59 (top icons), 59 (bottom icons); Robbie Shone/Science Source, 8–9; Thierry Berrod/Mona Lisa Production/Science Source, 12–13; John Pohlman/USGS, 24–25; Rowan Romeyn/Alamy, 26–27; NOAA/Nature Source/Science Source, 29; Martin Shields/Science Source, 32–33; Susan Montoya Bryan/AP Images, 34–35; Brent McGregor/AP Images, 36–37; Sergio Pitamitz/VWPics/Science Source, 38–39; British Antarctic Survey/Science Source, 40–41; Vincent Amouroux/Mona Lisa Production/Science Source, 46–47; Mert Gokhan Koc/Dia Images/AP Images, 49

Library of Congress Control Number: 2023922201

ISBN
979-8-89250-224-5 (hardcover)
979-8-89250-245-0 (paperback)
979-8-89250-284-9 (ebook pdf)
979-8-89250-266-5 (hosted ebook)

Printed in the United States of America
Mankato, MN
082024

NOTE TO PARENTS AND EDUCATORS

Apex books are designed to build literacy skills in striving readers. Exciting, high-interest content attracts and holds readers' attention. The text is carefully leveled to allow students to achieve success quickly.

TABLE OF CONTENTS

Chapter 1
STUDYING CAVES 4

Chapter 2
CAVE GEOLOGY 9

Chapter 3
WATER IN CAVES 18

That's Wild!
UNDER THE SEAFLOOR 28

Chapter 4
CAVE LIFE 30

Chapter 5
RISKS AND CHALLENGES 40

That's Wild!
CAVE RESCUE IN TURKEY 48

Chapter 6
TYPES OF TRAINING 50

SKILLS CHECKLIST • 59
COMPREHENSION QUESTIONS • 60
GLOSSARY • 62
TO LEARN MORE • 63
ABOUT THE AUTHOR • 63
INDEX • 64

Chapter 1

STUDYING CAVES

A group of scientists enters the mouth of a cave. It is very dark inside. The scientists turn on their headlamps. Their lights shine down the narrow tunnel.

Some plants live near the mouths of caves where there is more light.

Water drips from the tunnel's roof. It falls into a crack in the floor. A scientist shines her light there. She sees a deep hole. The scientists use ropes and harnesses to climb down it. They go deep underground. At the bottom, they discover a type of fish that has never been seen before.

BLIND FISH

A new kind of fish was found in a cave in China in 2022. The fish lives in the dark. It is blind and has no color. It also has a large horn sticking out of its head.

Using rope to go down a cliff or hole is called rappelling or abseiling.

Sediment is laid down in layers over time. Collecting it helps scientists learn about the past.

Chapter 2
CAVE GEOLOGY

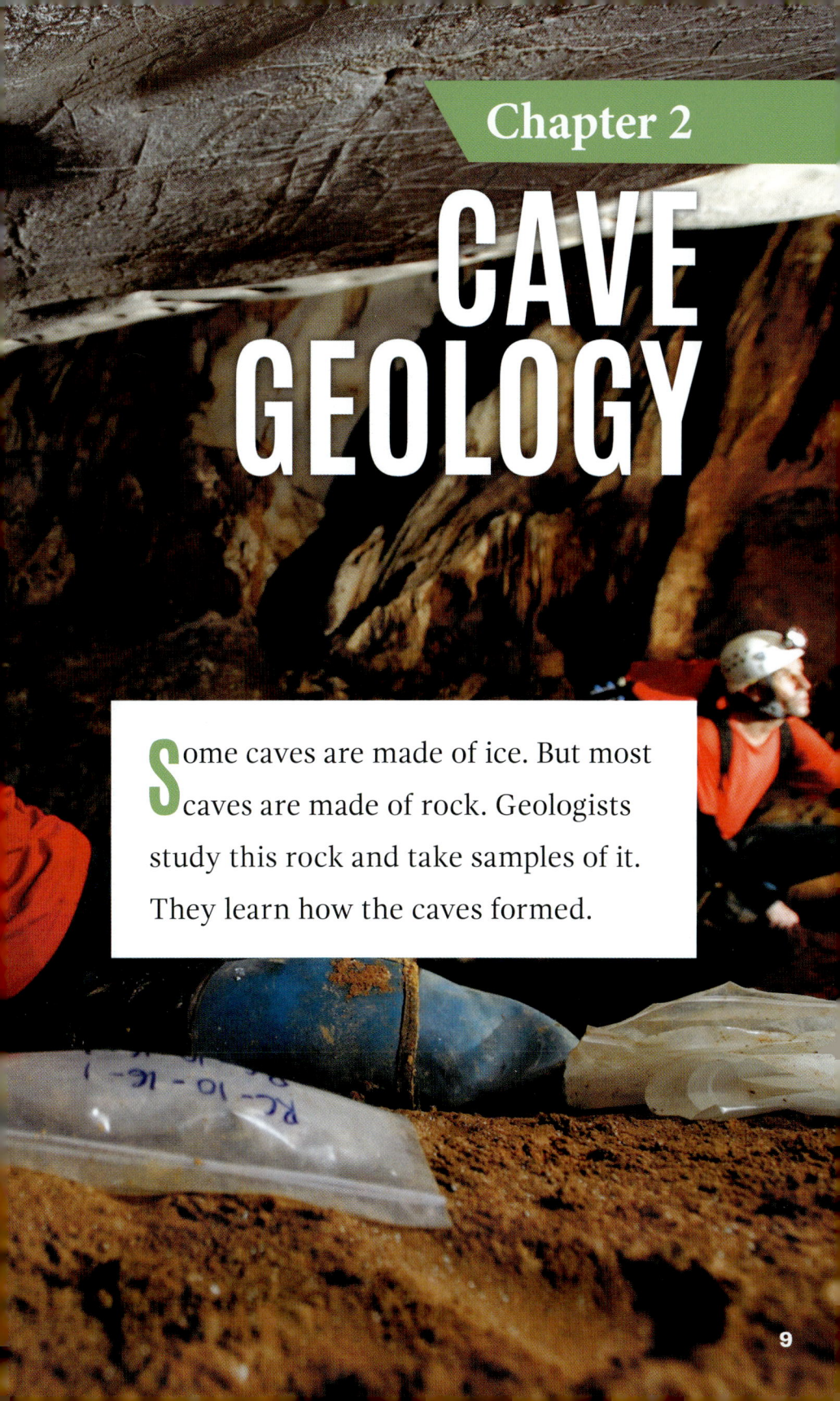

Some caves are made of ice. But most caves are made of rock. Geologists study this rock and take samples of it. They learn how the caves formed.

Most caves form because of erosion. For example, solution caves form underground. Rainwater gets into a crack in rock. Acids in the water dissolve the rock. More cracks form. The cracks grow over time. They eventually become a cave. Scientists look for entrances to solution caves. Then they go inside. They measure and map the caves.

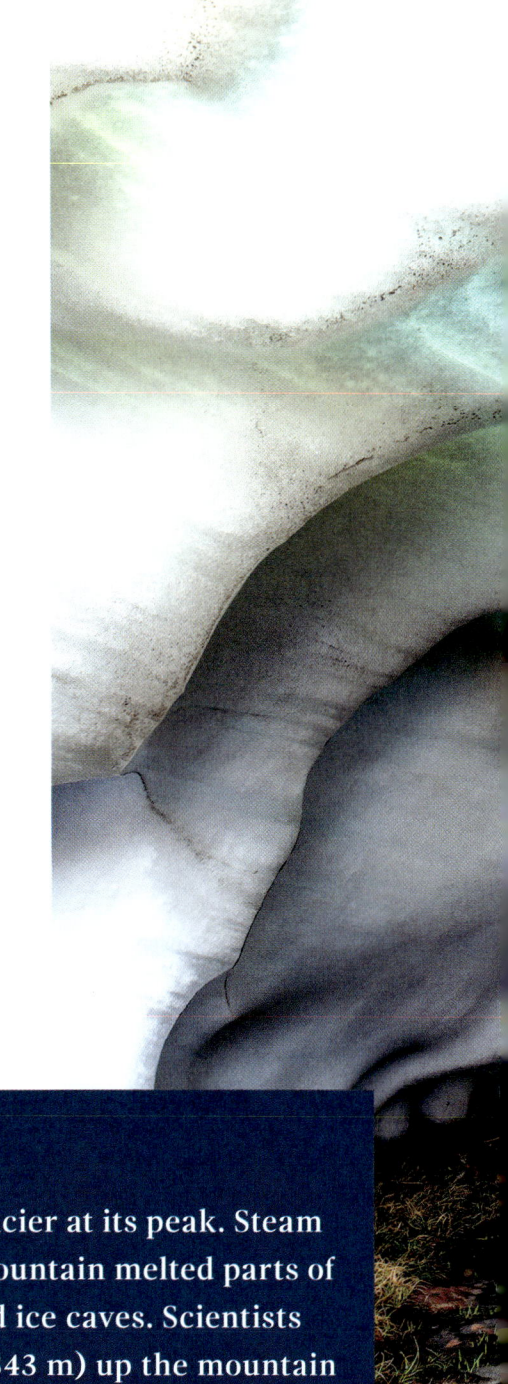

ICE CAVES

Mount Rainier has a glacier at its peak. Steam from deep inside the mountain melted parts of the glacier. This created ice caves. Scientists climbed 14,250 feet (4,343 m) up the mountain to study them.

Climate change has caused many ice caves on Mount Rainier to melt or become unstable.

Many caves are very old. They can be thousands of feet long. And they can have many spaces and tunnels. Scientists must take care not to get lost. They use maps. But caves continue to change and grow.

ROCK FORMATIONS

When rainwater drips in a cave, minerals are left behind. These create rock formations. Stalactites hang from the ceiling. Stalagmites grow up from the ground. Scientists sometimes cut stalagmites open. They study the rock layers to learn about the past.

Stalactites and stalagmites sometimes connect. They can form tall columns.

The Sea Lion Caves in Oregon are 1,315 feet (400 m) long.

Sea caves form near the edges of lakes or oceans. Waves crash into rocky cliffs. They wear away the rock over time. They carve rooms or passages. Scientists may take boats to study them.

TALUS CAVES

Some caves are formed from rocks falling. These are called talus caves. Large boulders fall to the bottom of a cliff. They pile on top of one another. The openings in between the rocks become caves. Rooms and tunnels form.

The islands of Hawai‘i have many caves made from lava.

Lava caves form after volcanoes erupt. As the lava flows, it slowly hardens. It forms a crust. Faster, hotter lava can move underneath this crust. This hot lava flows away. But the crust stays. A tube-shaped cave forms. Some caves are just one long tube. Others have many tunnels and branches. Scientists map and explore them.

LOTS OF LAVA

The world's longest lava cave is in Hawai'i. It stretches for more than 40 miles (64 km). And it goes more than 3,610 feet (1,100 m) under the ground.

Chapter 3
WATER IN CAVES

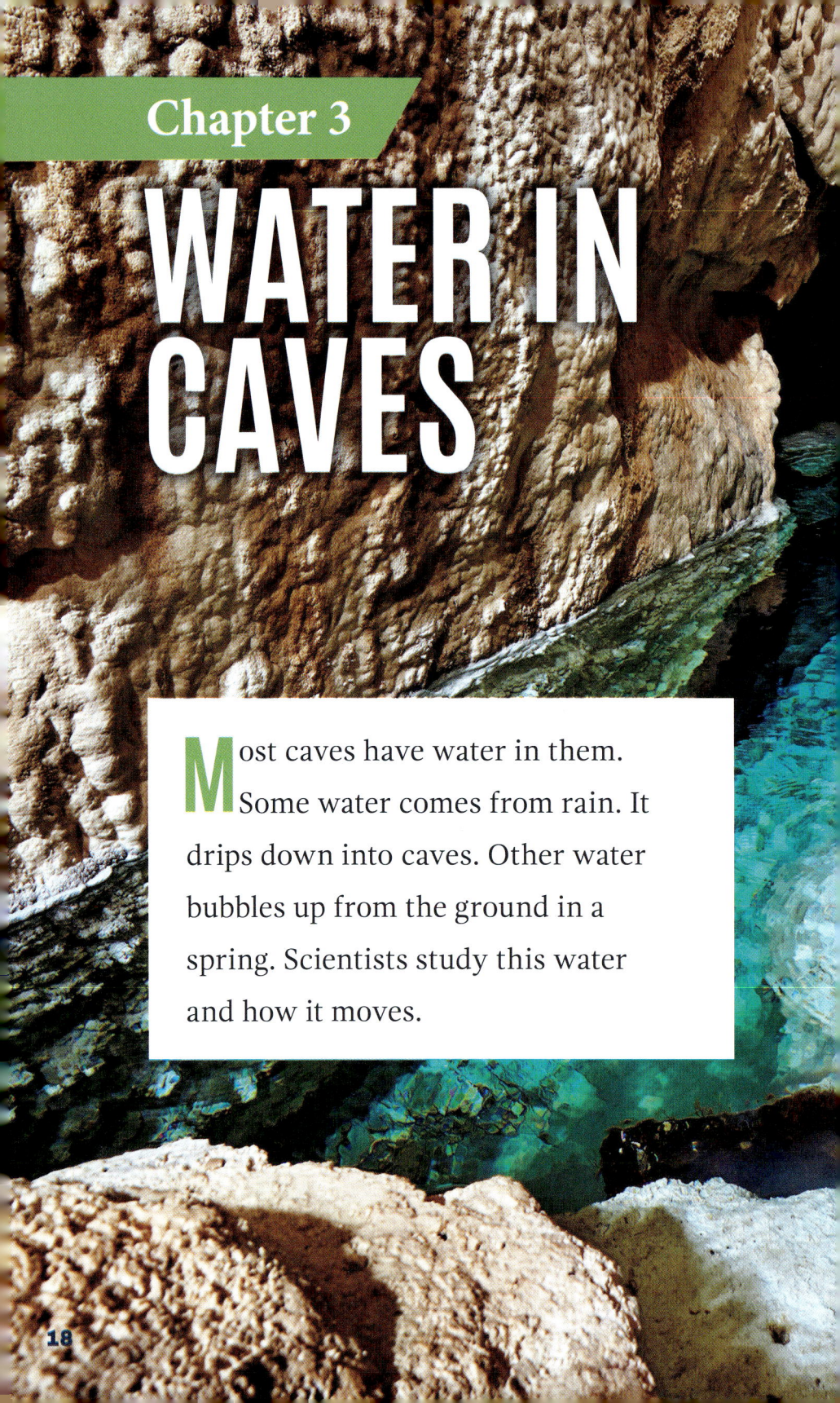

Most caves have water in them. Some water comes from rain. It drips down into caves. Other water bubbles up from the ground in a spring. Scientists study this water and how it moves.

Caves that have water dripping or flowing inside them are called active caves.

Mammoth Cave National Park has the world's longest cave system. Several streams and rivers flow into it.

Streams or rivers flow through some caves. In other caves, water drips through the rock. This water often flows into and out of surrounding areas. Scientists take samples of this water. They check it for pollution. They may also drop dye in or near caves. They look for where the colored water comes out. This can help them see where and how pollution spreads.

Caves can have underground lakes, too. The Veryovkina Cave is one example. It is the deepest cave in the world. It goes down 7,257 feet (2,212 m). Its bottom is filled with water. Scientists set up a camp near this lake. They found rare animals near the water.

ESCAPING A FLOOD

It takes scientists a week to climb to the bottom of Veryovkina Cave and back. So, they set up camps along the way. During one trip, the bottom camp flooded. Water roared through the cave. The scientists had to quickly reach a higher camp.

Križna Jama is a cave in Slovenia. It contains 22 underground lakes.

Some scientists dive in cenotes. This type of sinkhole forms when a cave's ceiling collapses.

Scientists dive to study some caves. They swim into deep sinkholes and underwater tunnels. They wear wet suits. And they breathe air from tanks. Scientists see how far the caves go. They also see what plants or animals live there.

UNREACHED SINKHOLE

The Zacatón sinkhole is in Mexico. It is more than 925 feet (282 m) deep. People have never reached its bottom. At least one diver has died trying to get there.

Parts of the Larsbreen ice cave are very narrow with high ceilings.

Scientists study water in ice caves, too. For example, Larsbreen is a glacier on Norway's Svalbard Islands. In the summer, melting water wears away its ice. Scientists use ropes to lower themselves into the cave. They map the twisting passages. They study how the melting water changes the glacier over time.

ANCIENT ICE

Caves deep underground can be very cold. Any water that comes inside freezes. Scientists take samples of this ice. They study its layers. This helps them learn what Earth's climate was like long ago.

That's Wild!
UNDER THE SEAFLOOR

In 2023, scientists studied deep-sea caves. They traveled to the Pacific Ocean. The caves there were more than 8,200 feet (2,500 m) beneath the ocean's surface. Scientists used a robot to explore them. The robot lifted pieces of lava rocks. Scientists found small caves filled with worms, snails, and other life. The caves were underneath hot vents. Scientists had known about life near hot vents. But this was the first time people found life underneath them.

Tube worms often live near places where water or gases rise from cracks in the seafloor.

29

Chapter 4
CAVE LIFE

Biologists study life in caves. Many creatures live in caves. They include bats, fish, and insects. Plants such as ferns and mosses live near cave entrances. But deeper inside, caves get very dark. Plants cannot grow.

Some caves are home to millions of bats.

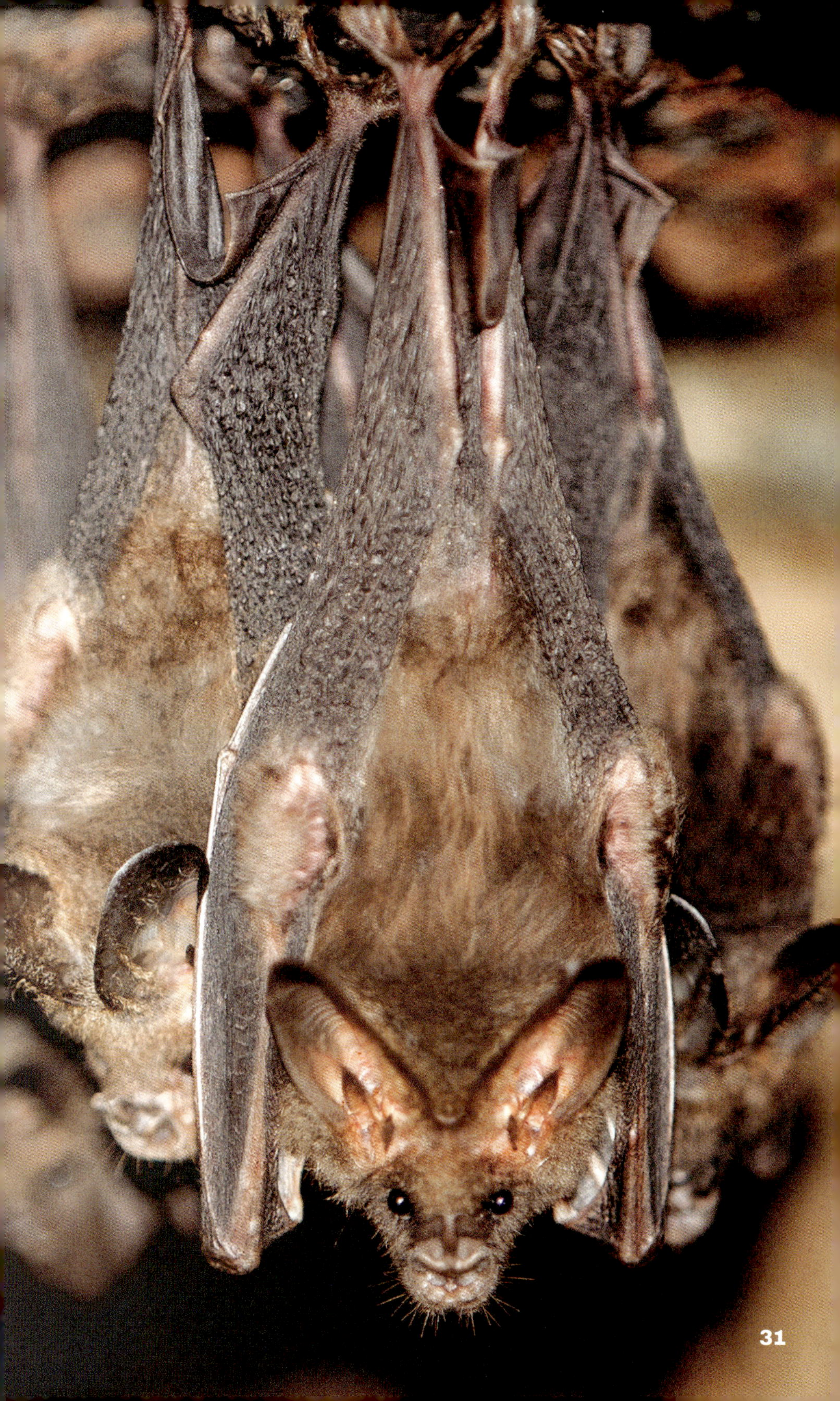

The blind cave fish is found in Central American caves.

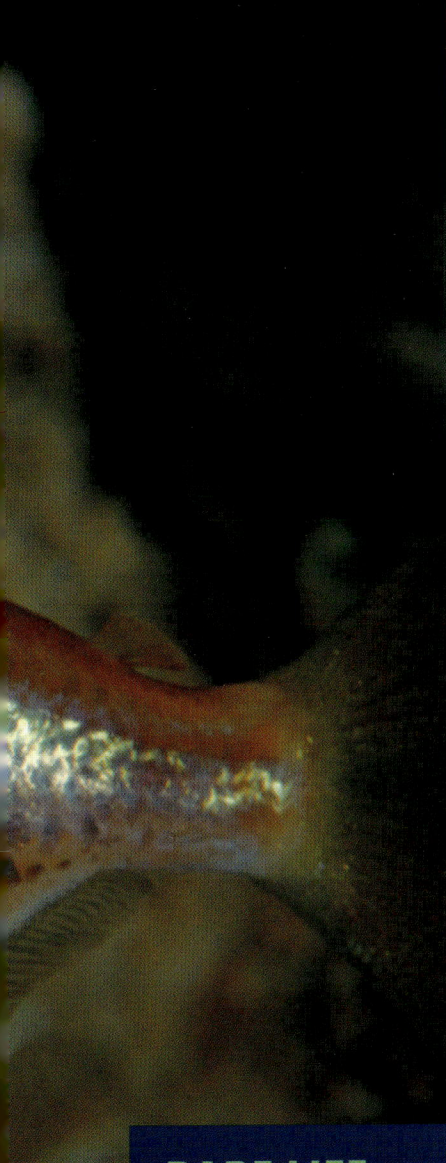

Some caves can be hot. Others are very cold. Most caves are damp. Cave creatures must live with little to no light. And food can be hard to find. Scientists study how animals adapt. For example, some cave fish have no eyes. Instead, cells in their skin sense movement. This helps the fish find food.

RARE LIFE

The United States has about 50,000 caves. More than 1,000 different kinds of plants and animals live in them. Many of these species can't live anywhere else.

Some scientists study microbes that live in caves. These tiny life-forms can live in extreme conditions. Some can survive high heat. Others can eat chemicals that would kill people. Scientists collect samples of microbes from rocks and water. They study how they survive.

SLIMY MICROBES

Cueva de Villa Luz is in Mexico. The cave has poisonous gas inside it. Microbes live in this toxic cave. They can be found on snottites. These are slimy tubes. They hang from the cave's ceiling.

Fort Stanton Cave is in New Mexico. Scientists found microbes living on its walls.

Scientists also look for new species. They travel deep into caves. One group explored caves in Israel. The group found seven new kinds of spiders. Researchers studied the spiders' DNA. They tried to learn how the spiders changed over time.

LEAVE NO TRACE

Many cave ecosystems are fragile. Even small changes could hurt them. So, scientists touch as little as possible. And they take all their supplies back out when they leave. This helps protect the caves.

In 2010, people found a new family of spiders in caves in Oregon. Scientists named it *Trogloraptor*, which means "cave robber."

Some caves contain fossils. Some fossils form when animals get trapped in caves. Others are revealed when water wears away rock. Scientists study fossils. They learn what plants and animals lived in or near the cave.

Scientists found fossils of a cave bear in Slovenia.

STUDYING HISTORY

Many cave researchers study the past. Some researchers study things that people left in caves thousands of years ago. They have found items such as bowls and sandals. These items help researchers understand how people lived long ago.

Chapter 5

RISKS AND CHALLENGES

Caves can be hard to get to. People may have to hike or take boats to reach them. Some caves are on high cliffs or are underwater. Plus, scientists may go deep into caves through narrow tunnels. Sending help can be difficult.

Scientists explore caves in Antarctica by climbing their icy walls.

Scientists wear hiking boots in wet caves so they don't slip and fall.

Caves are dark and damp. They may have many deep holes. Floors and walls can be slippery. People are at risk of falling.

LIVING UNDERGROUND

Some scientists stay in caves for many days. One woman lived alone in a cave for 500 days. She learned how living in the dark affects the body and mind.

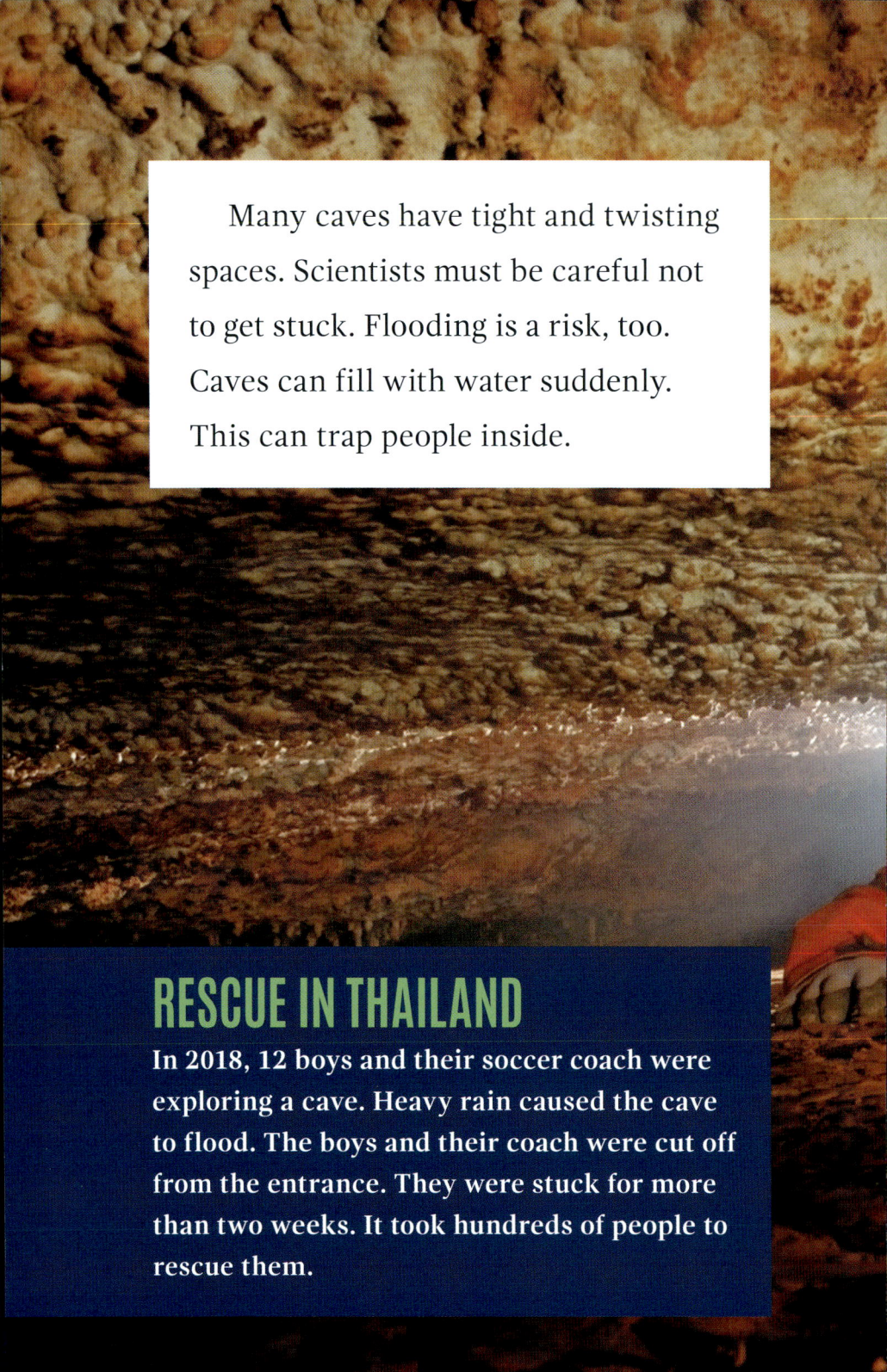

Many caves have tight and twisting spaces. Scientists must be careful not to get stuck. Flooding is a risk, too. Caves can fill with water suddenly. This can trap people inside.

RESCUE IN THAILAND

In 2018, 12 boys and their soccer coach were exploring a cave. Heavy rain caused the cave to flood. The boys and their coach were cut off from the entrance. They were stuck for more than two weeks. It took hundreds of people to rescue them.

People learn to relax and breathe slowly when moving through tight passages.

Scientists wear masks so they don't breathe in dangerous gases.

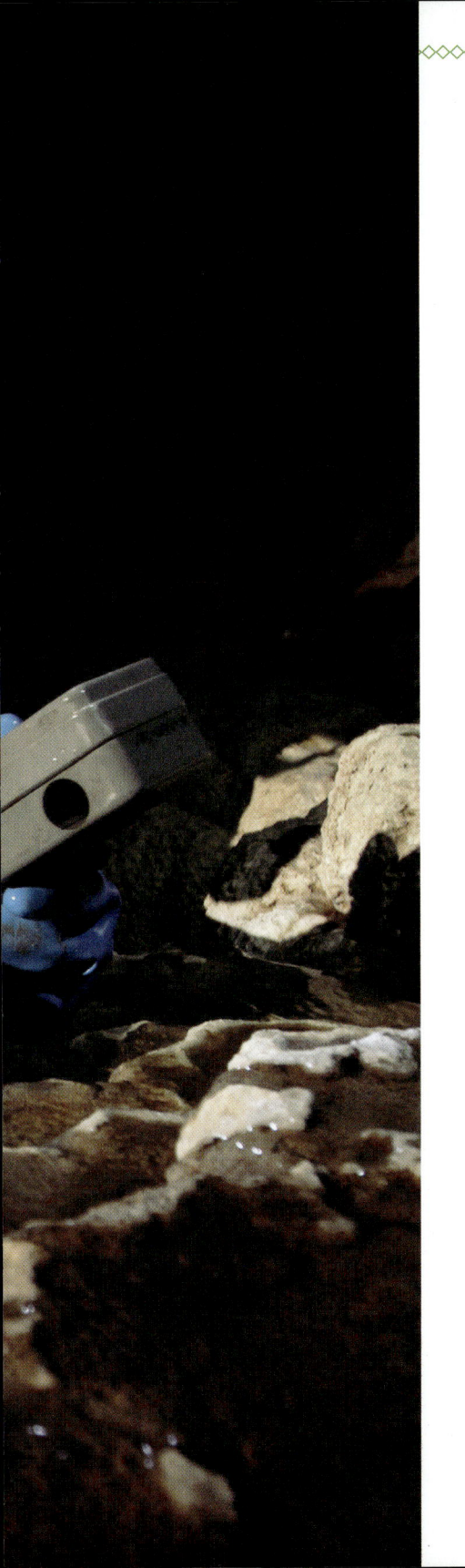

Dangerous gases can build up in caves. To stay safe, scientists test the air. They use kits and tools to check gas levels. If levels get too high, scientists must leave the cave quickly. Otherwise, they could get sick or die.

Caves can also be unstable. Rocks can fall at any time. Scientists wear helmets to protect their heads. A rockfall can block an exit. If that happens, scientists must find another way to get out.

That's Wild!

CAVE RESCUE IN TURKEY

In 2023, Mark Dickey visited one of the deepest caves in Turkey. He was mapping the cave. One day, he got sick. He was more than 3,280 feet (1,000 m) below the cave's entrance. He became too weak to climb. A doctor climbed down to care for him. Then rescuers came. They carried Dickey on a stretcher. It took them more than a week to bring him to the surface. They made many stops to rest along the way.

It took more than 200 people from five countries to rescue Mark Dickey.

49

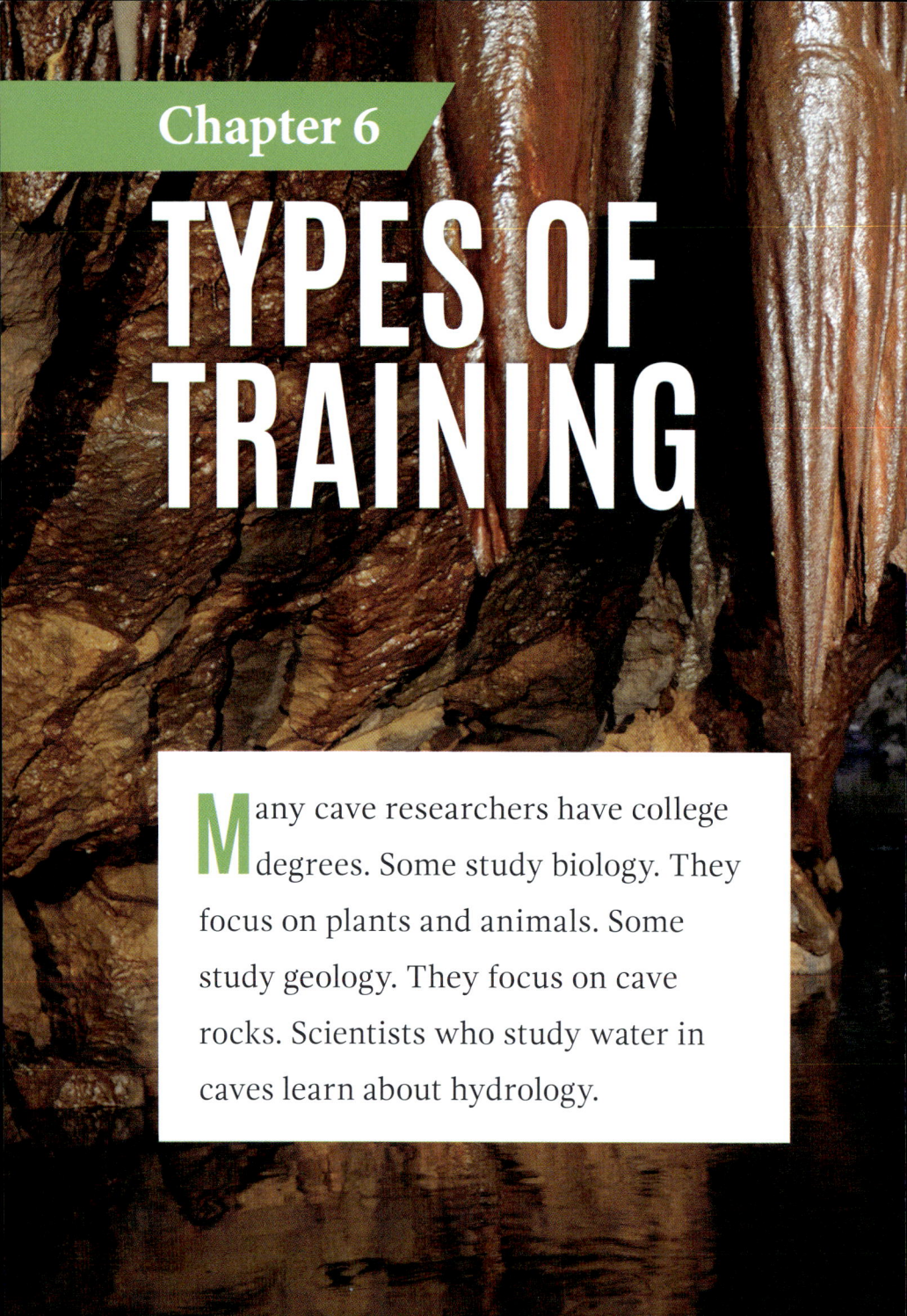

Chapter 6

TYPES OF TRAINING

Many cave researchers have college degrees. Some study biology. They focus on plants and animals. Some study geology. They focus on cave rocks. Scientists who study water in caves learn about hydrology.

The science of studying caves is called speleology.

Many caves have steep cliffs or deep holes. So, scientists learn to use ropes and harnesses. First, they lower themselves down. Brakes on the ropes stop them from falling too quickly. Then the scientists climb back up.

To stay safe, people should never climb alone. Instead, they work in groups.

ICE CLIMBING

The Booming Ice Chasm is in Canada. It has a 590-foot (180-m) sheet of clear ice. Scientists rappel down it. They study a frozen lake at the cave's bottom. Then they use ice picks to climb back to the surface.

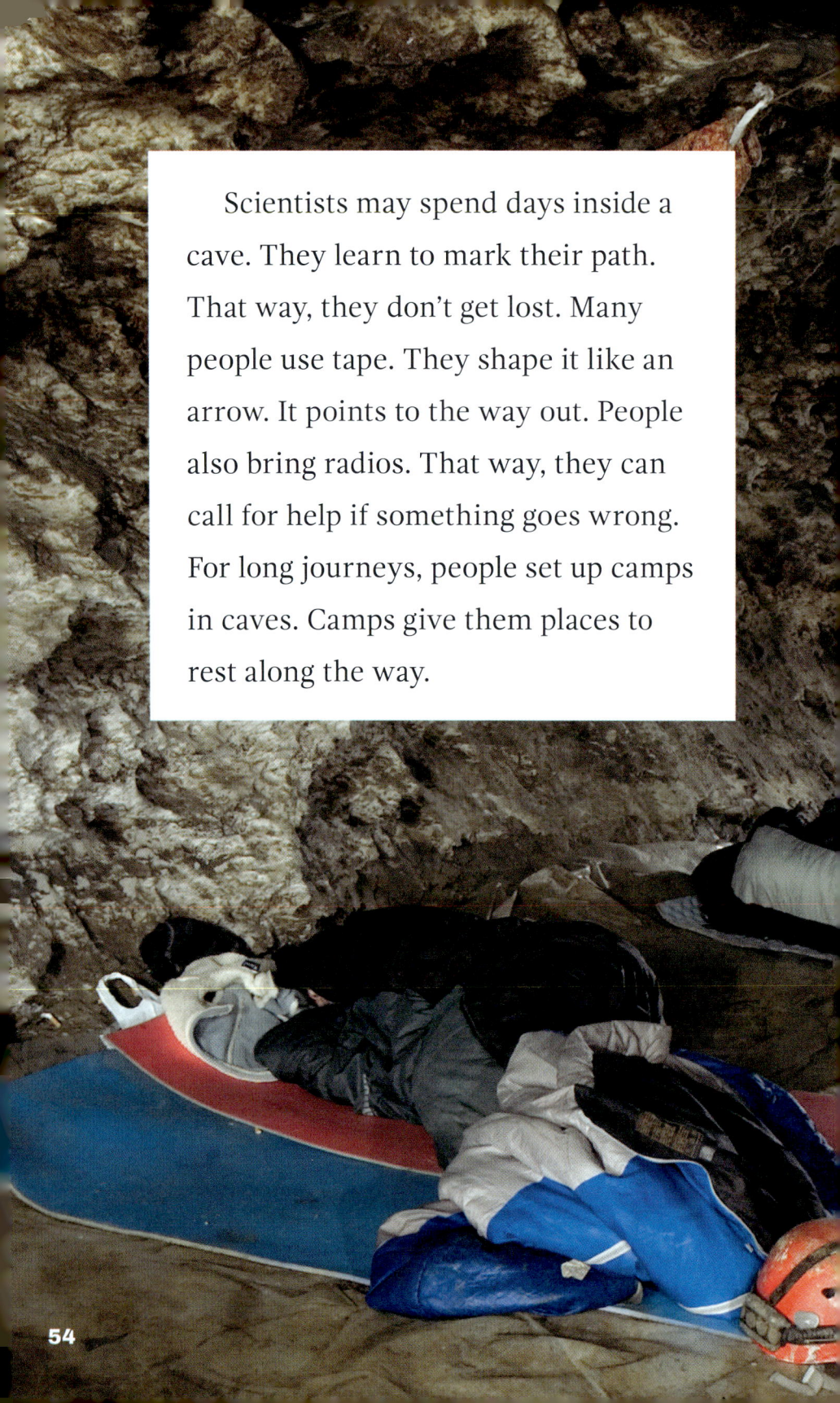

Scientists may spend days inside a cave. They learn to mark their path. That way, they don't get lost. Many people use tape. They shape it like an arrow. It points to the way out. People also bring radios. That way, they can call for help if something goes wrong. For long journeys, people set up camps in caves. Camps give them places to rest along the way.

During long stays in caves, people may use tents or sleeping bags.

CAVE RESCUE IN GERMANY

Johann Westhauser was exploring Germany's deepest cave in 2014. Rocks fell on him and hurt him badly. He was 4 miles (6.4 km) from the cave's entrance. Hundreds of people worked to rescue him. It took 12 days to bring him to the surface.

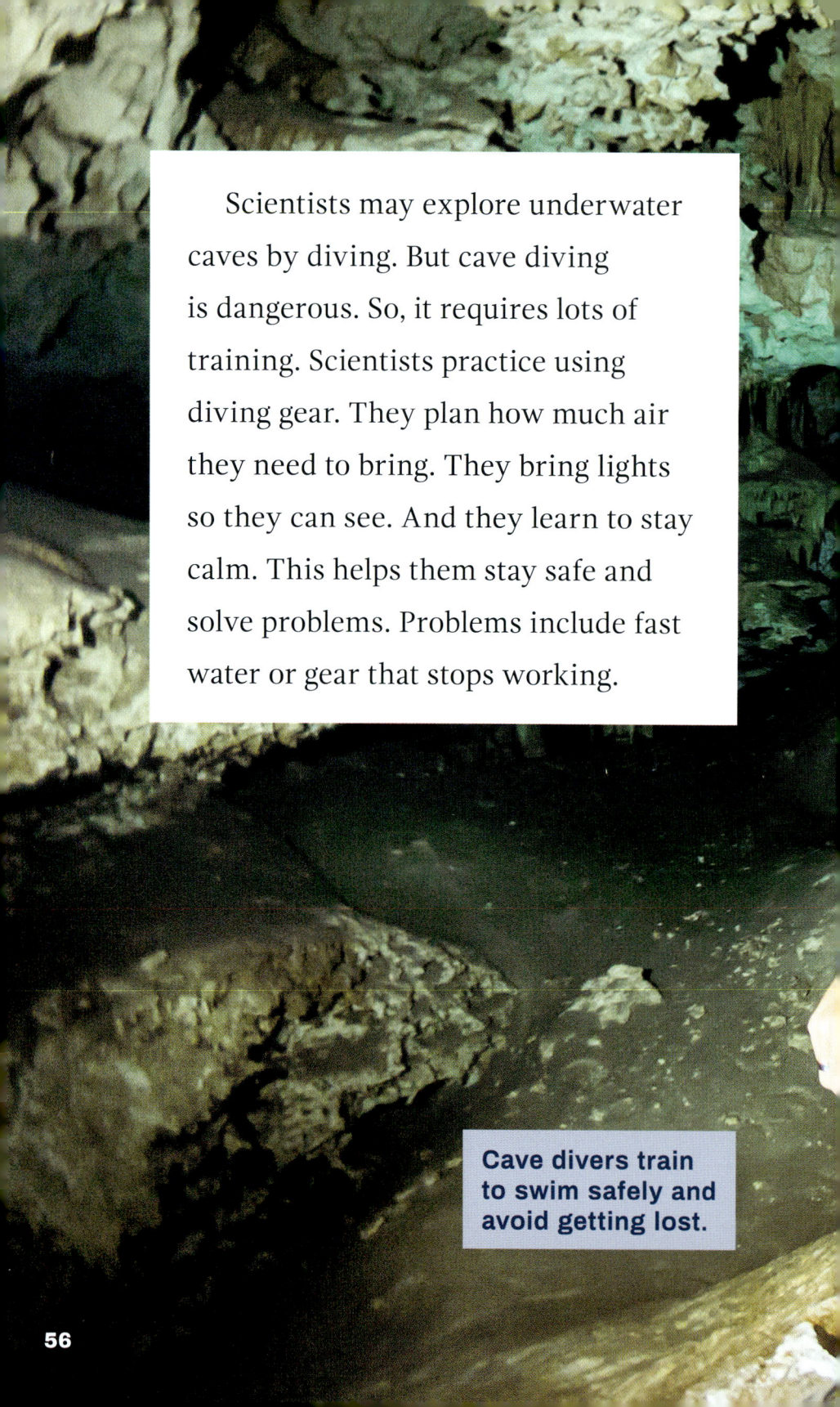

Scientists may explore underwater caves by diving. But cave diving is dangerous. So, it requires lots of training. Scientists practice using diving gear. They plan how much air they need to bring. They bring lights so they can see. And they learn to stay calm. This helps them stay safe and solve problems. Problems include fast water or gear that stops working.

Cave divers train to swim safely and avoid getting lost.

57

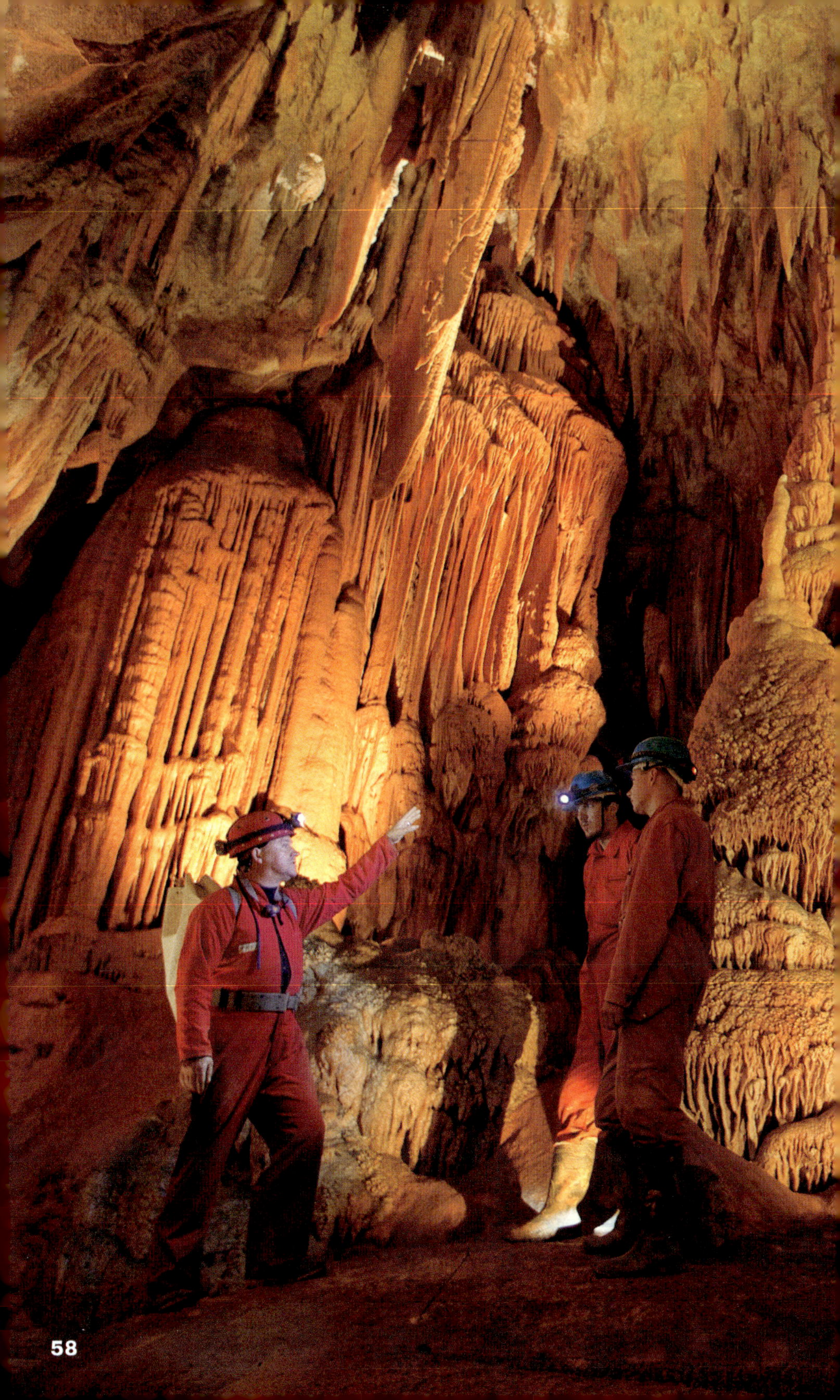

✓ SKILLS CHECKLIST

TYPES OF SCIENCE

- Biology
- Geology
- Hydrology

OUTDOOR ACTIVITIES

- Camping
- Diving
- Mapmaking
- Navigating
- Rock and Ice Climbing

COMPREHENSION QUESTIONS

Write your answers on a separate piece of paper.

1. Write a few sentences about how scientists travel inside caves.

2. Would you want to travel deep inside a cave? Why or why not?

3. How many different kinds of plants and animals live in US caves?

    A. fewer than 50
    B. about 800
    C. more than 1,000

4. Why would scientists want to learn how pollution spreads in and near caves?

    A. so they can plan how to help it spread less
    B. so they can plan how to spread it more
    C. so they can go to new areas

5. What does **eventually** mean in this book?

The cracks grow over time. They eventually become a cave.

    A. never
    B. at a later time
    C. right away

6. What does **fragile** mean in this book?

Many cave ecosystems are fragile. Even small changes could hurt them.

    A. not possible to break or hurt
    B. easy to break or hurt
    C. very tiny

Answer key on page 64.

GLOSSARY

acids
Strong chemicals that can break down or wear away the things they touch.

ecosystems
Groups of living things and their environments.

erosion
When something slowly wears away over time.

fossils
Remains of plants and animals that lived long ago.

glacier
A large, slow-moving body of ice.

lava
Hot, melted rock that flows along Earth's surface.

microbes
Tiny living things, such as bacteria.

pollution
Things that are dirty or unsafe.

rappel
To use ropes to climb down something.

species
Groups of animals or plants that are similar and can breed with one another.

vents
Openings where gas, steam, or liquid leaves the ground.

TO LEARN MORE
BOOKS
Rathburn, Betsy. *Exploring Caves*. Minneapolis: Bellwether Media, 2023.

Romero, Libby. *Cool Caves*. New York: DK Publishing, 2023.

Soontornvat, Christina. *All Thirteen: The Incredible Cave Rescue of the Thai Boys' Soccer Team*. Somerville, MA: Candlewick Press, 2020.

ONLINE RESOURCES
Visit **www.apexeditions.com** to find links and resources related to this title.

ABOUT THE AUTHOR
Julie Kentner is a writer who loves to read. She studied archaeology in university. She lives in Winnipeg, Manitoba, Canada with her husband and their cats.

INDEX

animals, 22, 25, 33, 38, 50

camps, 22, 54
Cueva de Villa Luz, 34

diving, 25, 56

erosion, 10

fish, 6, 30, 33
flooding, 22, 44
fossils, 38

gases, 34, 47
glaciers, 10, 27

ice, 9–10, 27, 53

lakes, 15, 22, 53
lava caves, 17

microbes, 34

plants, 25, 30, 33, 38, 50
pollution, 21

rain, 10, 13, 18, 44
rescues, 44, 48, 55
rocks, 9–10, 13, 15, 21, 28, 34, 38, 47, 50, 55
ropes, 6, 27, 52

sea caves, 15
sinkholes, 25
solution caves, 10
stalactites, 13
stalagmites, 13

talus caves, 15
tunnels, 4, 6, 12, 15, 17, 25, 40

Veryovkina Cave, 22

water, 6, 10, 13, 18, 21–22, 25, 27, 34, 38, 40, 44, 50, 56

Zacatón, 25

ANSWER KEY:
1. Answers will vary; 2. Answers will vary; 3. C; 4. A; 5. B; 6. B